Craft Stick MANIA

Christine M. Irvin

Children's Press®

A Division of Scholastic Inc.

New York • Toronto • London • Auckland • Sydney

Mexico City • New Delhi • Hong Kong

Danbury, Connecticut

The author and publisher are not responsible for injuries or accidents that occur during or from any craft projects. Craft projects should be conducted in the presence of or with the help of an adult. Any instructions of the craft projects that require the use of sharp or other unsafe items should be conducted by or with the help of an adult.

Design and Production by Function Thru Form Inc.
Illustrations by Mia Gomez, Function Thru Form Inc.
Photographs ©: School Tools/Joe Atlas

Library of Congress Cataloging-in-Publication Data

Irvin, Christine M.
    Craft stick mania / by Christine M. Irvin
      p. cm. — (Craft mania)
    Includes index.
    ISBN 0-516-21676-7 (lib. bdg.)   0-516-27757-X (pbk.)
    1. Handicraft—Juvenile literature. 2. Staffs (Sticks, canes, etc.)—Juvenile literature.
    [1. Handicraft.] I. Title. II. Series.

    TT880 .I79 2001
    745.51—dc21

                          00-065643

CHILDREN'S PRESS and associated logos are trademarks and or registered trademarks of Grolier Publishing Co., Inc.
SCHOLASTIC and associated logos are trademarks and or registered trademarks of Scholastic Inc.

1 2 3 4 5 6 7 8 9 10 R 11 10 09 08 07 06 05 04 03 02

Table of Contents

Welcome to the World of
CRAFT MANIA!

Don't throw away those ice cream sticks! Everyday items, such as ice cream sticks and paper plates, can become exciting works of art. You can have fun doing the projects and help save the environment at the same time by recycling these household objects instead of just throwing them away.

You can find ways to reuse many things around your home in craft projects. Bottle caps, buttons, old dried beans, and seeds can become eyes, ears, or a nose for an animal. Instead of buying construction paper, you can use scraps of wrapping paper or even last Sunday's comics to cover your art projects. Save the twist ties from bags of bread or vegetables—they make great legs! These are just a few examples of how you can turn garbage into art. Try to think of other things in your home that can be used in your crafts.

Did You Know?

- Each person creates about 4 pounds (1.8 kilograms) of garbage per day.

- Each person in the United States uses about 580 pounds (260 kg) of paper every year. Businesses in the United States use enough paper to circle the earth 20 times every day!

- Americans use enough cardboard each year to make a paper bale as big as a football field.

- Americans throw away more than 60 billion food and drink cans (like tin cans and soft drink cans) and 28 billion glass bottles and jars (like those from ketchup and pickles) every year.

That's a lot of trash!

What you will need

It's easy to get started on your craft projects. The crafts in this book require some materials you can find around your home, some basic art supplies, and your imagination.

Buttons, bottle caps, beads, old dried beans or seeds for decoration

Glue

Tape

Tempera paints

Colored markers

Hole puncher

Construction paper (or newspaper or scraps of wrapping paper)

Felt (or scraps of fabric)

Twist ties (or pipe cleaners)

You might want to keep your craft materials in a box so that they will be ready any time you want to start a craft project. Now that you know what you need, look through the book and pick a project to try. Become a Craft Maniac!

A Note to Grown-Ups

Older children will be able to do most of the projects by themselves. Younger ones will need more adult supervision. All of them will enjoy making the items and playing with their finished creations. The directions for some of the crafts in this book require the use of scissors. Do not allow young children to use scissors without adult supervision.

👉 Helpful Hints

Save the different sized plastic and wooden sticks that come from frozen treats. These sticks can also be found in craft stores in many different sizes and colors. Tacky glue works best with craft sticks. It dries quickly and does not slip and slide as much as other glues.

Dragonfly

What you need

- **Three craft sticks**
- **Glue**
- **Pencil**
- **Tempera paints**
- **Paintbrush**
- **Two small beads or seeds**

What you do

1 Put wings on the dragonfly. Glue the three craft sticks together with two of the sticks placed across the third one as shown.

2 Decorate your dragonfly. Use the pencil to draw a design on the dragonfly's wings and body. Paint with tempera paints. Let the paint dry before going on to Step 3.

3 Finish your dragonfly. Glue on small beads or seeds for eyes.

Other Ideas

- Turn your dragonfly into an ornament. Make a loop out of string and glue it to the back of the dragonfly's head.

- Make an assortment of dragonflies, each a different color, and make each into an ornament. Hang the dragonflies in front of a window for a pretty display.

- Use glitter glue or markers to decorate your dragonfly instead of paint.

Coaster

What you need

- Fourteen craft sticks
- Glue

What you do

 Arrange two craft sticks about 4½ inches apart (the length of one craft stick).

 Put glue on both ends of a third craft stick. Press it in place on the ends of the other two craft sticks, as shown.

3 Glue a fourth craft stick in place beside the third one. Continue gluing craft sticks side-by-side until the bottom two craft sticks are covered, as shown. Let the glue dry.

Stick People

What you need

- One craft stick for each person
- Markers
- Bits of material for clothes
- Bits of yarn for hair
- Scissors (Before cutting any material, please ask an adult for help.)
- Glue

What you do

1 Make the face. Glue scraps of yarn around the top edge of the stick for hair, as shown, or draw the hair with a marker. Draw in eyes, eyebrows, nose, and mouth.

2 Dress your person. Cut and glue scraps of material to the stick for clothing. Let the glue dry before playing with your stick person.

Other Ideas

- Use very small beads for tiny buttons on the clothes.

- Add arms to your people. Glue a pipe cleaner to the back of the stick so that it sticks out on both sides for arms.

- Use your stick people as finger puppets. Glue a loop of paper to the back of each stick person. Make the loop big enough to slide your finger through.

Fish Trivet

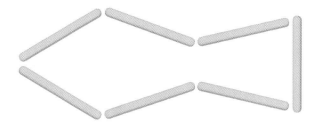

What you need

- Seven craft sticks
- Glue
- One small bean or button

What you do

1 Arrange the craft sticks in the shape of a fish, as shown.

 Glue the sticks together. Put a small drop of glue on the end of each stick and glue the sticks together in the fish shape, overlapping the edges, as shown.

3 Add an eye. Glue on a small bean or button for a fish eye.

Let the glue dry before using your trivet.

That's it!

Other Ideas

- Decorate your fish trivet. Paint with tempera paints or color with markers.

- Make a set of trivets and give it as a present. Paint each fish a different color.

Bookworm Bookmark

What you need

- One craft stick
- Tempera paints
- Paintbrush
- One small cotton ball
- Glue
- Two small seeds or beads

What you do

1 Decorate your craft stick. Paint the craft stick with tempera paints. Use your own design. Let the paint dry before going on to Step 2.

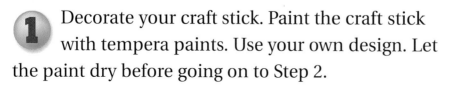

2 Make a head for your bookworm. Put a small drop of glue on the back of the cotton ball. Stick it on the craft stick for a head, as shown.

3 Add eyes. Glue two small seeds for eyes. Let the glue dry before using your bookmark.

My Story Book

Other Ideas

- Decorate the body of your bookworm with markers or crayons instead of tempera paints.

- Add a bit of glitter to make your bookworm sparkle.

- Glue a magnet to the back of the bookworm and use it for a refrigerator magnet.

- Turn your bookworm into a caterpillar by adding a twist tie for an antenna.

Snowflake

- Six craft sticks
- Glue
- Tempera paints
- Paintbrush
- Glitter or glitter glue
- One piece of ribbon or string

What you do

1 Make the first part of the snowflake. Use two sticks. Put a drop of glue in the middle of each stick and press together, as shown. Let the glue dry before going on to Step 2.

2 Glue the rest of the craft sticks to the snowflake. Put a drop of glue on the end of one of the remaining sticks. Press the stick onto one corner of the center of the snowflake, as shown. Glue all four of the sticks to the snowflake, one on each corner. The ends of the sticks will touch each other in the middle of the snowflake. Let the glue dry before going on to Step 3.

18

3 Paint your snowflake with tempera paints. Let the paint dry before going on to Step 4.

4 Spread a thin layer of glue around the surface of the snowflake. Sprinkle glitter onto the glue. Let the glue dry. Turn the snowflake over, and tap the extra glitter off of it.

5 Make your snowflake an ornament. Glue a loop of ribbon onto one of the ends of the snowflake. Now it is ready to be hung up.

Other Ideas

- Use different colors of glitter on your snowflake.
- Glue a magnet to the back of your snowflake and stick it on the refrigerator.
- Make several snowflakes. Hang them in front of a window for a seasonal decoration.

Pencil Holder

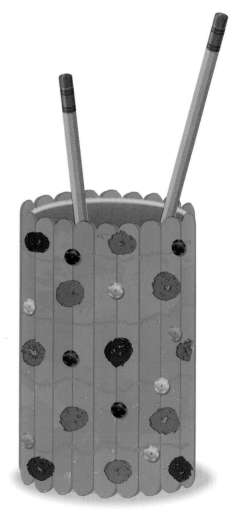

What you need

- One empty soup can, clean and dry
- Twenty to twenty-five craft sticks, depending on size of can
- Glue
- Tempera paints
- Paintbrush

What you do

1 Paint the soup can with tempera paints. Painting the can prevents the label from showing through when you are finished. Wait for the paint to dry before going on to Step 2.

2 Glue the craft sticks around the outside of the soup can. Spread a thin layer of glue along one side of the craft stick. Press it to the side of the can, as shown. Make sure the first stick is straight before gluing the next one. Glue on one craft stick at a time until you have gone all the way around the can. Let the glue dry before using your pencil holder.

That's it! Your pencil holder is ready to use!

Other Ideas

- Paint your craft sticks with tempera paints.
- You can even use your pencil holder can as a flower vase.

Jumping Frog

What you need

- **Eleven craft sticks**
- **Glue**
- **Marker**

What you do

1 Make the frog's body. Glue two craft sticks together side-by-side by spreading glue on the edge of one craft stick and pressing another craft stick to the glue. Spread glue on the flat side of another craft stick. Press the craft stick in place on top of the other two craft sticks, as shown. Set the body aside and let the glue dry.

Make the frog's legs. Glue two craft sticks together at an angle, as shown, to make one leg. Make three more legs the same way. Let the glue dry before going on to Step 3.

 Put your frog together. Turn the frog's body over. Place a small drop of glue on the end of one leg. Glue the leg in place on the frog's body, as shown. Glue the other three legs in place, as shown. Let the glue dry before going on to Step 4.

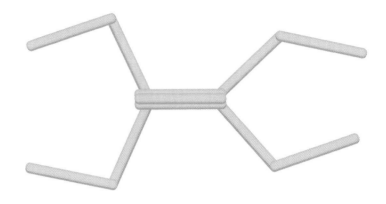

Draw in eyes with a marker.

Other Ideas

- Paint the craft sticks before gluing them together.
- Glue magnets to the back of the frog's body to make a refrigerator magnet.

Spooky Spiderweb

What you need

- **Three craft sticks**
- **Yarn**
- **Scissors** (Before cutting any material, please ask an adult for help.)
- **Glue**

What you do

1 Make a frame for your web. Put a small drop of glue in the middle of a craft stick. Press another craft stick on the glue so the two craft sticks make an "X." Put a small drop of glue in the middle of the third craft stick. Press it in place on top of the first two craft sticks, like the spokes of a wheel, as shown. Let the glue dry before going on to Step 2.

2 Attach the yarn to the craft sticks. Tie one end of the yarn around the middle of the web frame, as shown.

3 Make the web. Wrap the other end of the yarn around the first spoke to the right, as shown.

Continue wrapping the yarn around the craft stick spokes until you have covered the whole web, as shown. Have an adult help you cut the end of the yarn. Secure the end of the yarn with a small drop of glue on the back of the last spoke. Let the glue dry before playing with your web.

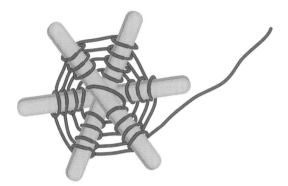

Other Ideas

- Paint the craft sticks with tempera paints before you glue them together.

- Make a spooky spider for your web. Have an adult help you cut a small circle from a piece of construction paper. Glue short pieces of pipe cleaners or twist ties to the construction paper for the legs. Add eyes with a marker or glue on small beads or seeds.

Trinket Box

What you need

- About twenty-six craft sticks
- Glue

What you do

1 Start the base of the box. Arrange two craft sticks about 4½ inches apart (the length of one craft stick). Put small drops of glue on both ends of a third craft stick. Press it in place on the ends of the other two craft sticks, as shown.

2 Finish the base. Glue another craft stick in place beside that one, as shown. Continue gluing crafts sticks side-by-side until the bottom two craft sticks are covered. Let the glue dry before going on to Step 2.

3 Build the first row of the trinket box's sides. Spread glue on the flat side of a craft stick. Press it in place on one edge of the base, as shown. Glue another craft stick on the opposite edge of the base.

4 Build the second row. Glue two crafts sticks across the ends of the first row, as shown.

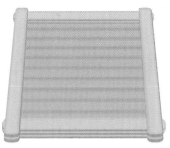

5 Add another row. Glue two more craft sticks the same way you did for the first row. Continue adding craft sticks in this manner until your trinket box is as deep as you want it. Let the glue dry before using your trinket box.

Other Ideas

- Before you glue the craft sticks together, paint them different colors.

- Make a lid for your trinket box by following the directions for the base. The finished base can then be used as a lid.

Picture Frame

What you need

- Twent-one craft sticks
- Glue
- Waxed paper
- One piece of string 12 inches long
- One piece of cardboard, like the kind that comes with shirts
- Tape
- Scissors (Before cutting material, please ask an adult for help.)

What you do

1 Make the sides for the frame. For each side of the frame, glue four craft sticks edge to edge on a piece of waxed paper, as shown. Leave the sticks on the waxed paper until the glue dries. When the glue is dry, you can remove the sticks from the paper. Make four sides. Let the glue dry before going on to Step 2.

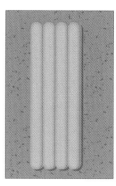

Make the frame. Arrange the four sides to make a square shape. Overlap and glue the sticks together at the corners, as shown. Let the glue dry before going on to Step 3.

3 Make a space for a photograph. Glue two more craft sticks stacked on top of each other on one edge of the frame. Glue two more craft sticks on top of the edge directly across from the first stack. Glue one craft stick on one of the edges between the two stacks.

4 Put a backing on your frame. Have an adult help you cut the cardboard into a 4½-inch by 6½-inch rectangle. Glue the cardboard to three sides on the back of the frame, as shown. Let the glue dry.

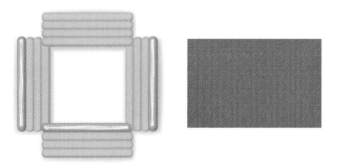

5 Tape string to the back of the cardboard. All you need is your favorite 4-inch by 6-inch picture and you are ready to hang your frame on the wall.

Other Ideas

- Experiment with the craft sticks, arranging them in different ways for different frame shapes.
- Paint your photo frame with tempera paints.

Tissue Paper Kite

- **Four craft sticks**
- **Small piece of tissue paper**
- **Pencil**
- **Scissors** (Before cutting any material, please ask an adult for help.)
- **Glue**
- **Two straws**
- **One 18-inch piece of string or yarn**

What you do

1 Make a kite frame. Arrange the craft sticks in a diamond shape. Place a small amount of glue on both ends of each stick. Glue the sticks together, overlapping the edges, as shown. Let the glue dry before going on to Step 2.

30

2 Cut out the tissue paper. Lay the kite frame on top of the tissue paper. Use the pencil to trace around the outside edges of the frame, as shown. Have an adult help you cut the tissue paper along the lines.

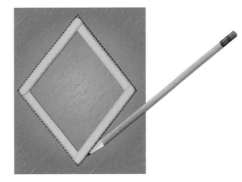

3 Spread a thin layer of glue around the kite frame. Attach the tissue paper on the kite frame. Be careful to keep the edges straight. Press the paper into place on the glue.

4 Add supports. Glue the straws across the back of the kite, as shown. Cut the ends off the straws if they stick out past the edges of the kite frame.

5 Add a tail. Put a small drop of glue on one corner of the kite. Glue the string on for the tail.

Other Ideas

- Paint the frame of the kite with tempera paints.

- Put bows on the tail of your kite. Tie knots in the tail every 3 to 4 inches. Tie short pieces of ribbon tightly above each knot.

- Make an assortment of kites to hang on your bedroom wall.

Index

About the Author

Christine M. Irvin lives in the Columbus, Ohio area with her husband, her three children, and her dog. She enjoys writing, reading, doing arts and crafts, and shopping.